W9-BFB-323

RAPTORS!

VULTURES

Liz Chung

PowerKiDS press.

New York

Published in 2016 by The Rosen Publishing Group, Inc.
29 East 21st Street, New York, NY 10010

First Edition

Editor: Sarah Machajewski
Book Design: Mickey Harmon

Photo Credits: Cover (series logo) Elena Paletskaya/Shutterstock.com; cover, pp. 1, 3–4, 6, 8, 10, 12, 14, 16, 18, 20, 22–24 (border texture, fact box) Picsfive/Shutterstock.com; cover (background scene) Cristina Guidi/Shutterstock.com; cover (both vultures) Andrea Izzotti/Shutterstock.com; p. 5 William Gray/AWL Images/Getty Images; p. 7 (buzzard) Piotr Krzeslak/Shutterstock.com; p. 7 (owl) Philip Ellard/Shutterstock.com; p. 7 (falcon, hawk) Chris Hill/Shutterstock.com; p. 7 (eagle) Peter Wey/Shutterstock.com; p. 7 (vulture) Carmine Arienzo/Shutterstock.com; p. 9 (griffon vulture) StockPhotoAstur/Shutterstock.com; p. 9 (turkey vulture) Angel DiBilio/Shutterstock.com; pp. 9 (Andean condor), 22 Iakov Filimonov/Shutterstock.com; p. 9 (California condor) kojihirano/Shutterstock.com; p. 11 Alta Oosthuizen/Shutterstock.com; p. 12 Shanti Hesse/Shutterstock.com; p. 13 Ammit Jack/Shutterstock.com; p. 15 Mogens Trolle/Shutterstock.com; p. 17 Chad Wright Photography/Shutterstock.com; p. 19 Jay Ondreicka/Shutterstock.com. p. 21 James DeBoer/Shutterstock.com.

Library of Congress Cataloging-in-Publication Data

Chung, Liz.
  Vultures / Liz Chung.
      pages cm. — (Raptors!)
  Includes index.
  ISBN 978-1-5081-4254-6 (pbk.)
  ISBN 978-1-5081-4255-3 (6 pack)
  ISBN 978-1-5081-4273-7 (library binding)
  1. Vultures—Juvenile literature. I. Title.
  QL696.F32C484 2016
  598.9'2—dc23
                                    2015036311

Manufactured in the United States of America

CPSIA Compliance Information: Batch #BW16PK: For Further Information contact Rosen Publishing, New York, New York at 1-800-237-9932

Contents

Dead Meat

Raptors are birds that are carnivores, which means they eat only meat. Most raptors catch **prey** that's living, but one raptor is known for having a taste for the dead stuff. It's the vulture.

Vultures don't have a very good **reputation**. They're **scavengers** that prey on weak, sick, and dead animals. They're not exactly the prettiest birds. But don't let that fool you—vultures are very important and really cool, too.

> Many people feel the way vultures look matches the way they act. What do you think?

A Closer Look at Raptors

Raptors are different from most birds. There are 10,000 species, or kinds, of birds in the world, but only a few species are raptors. If a bird eats meat, it's a raptor. Raptors also have great eyesight. They have a sharp, hooked beak and sharp claws, which are called talons.

Vultures are raptors because they have all these features. Eagles, owls, falcons, hawks, and buzzards are raptors, too.

RAPTOR FACTOR

"Bird of prey" is another name for a raptor.

falcon

eagle

owl

hawk

buzzard

vulture

These birds look a little different, but the features they share make each of them a raptor.

A Closer Look at Vultures

The name "vulture" is used for two groups of scavenging birds—Old World vultures and New World vultures. Old World vultures include the griffon vulture and hooded vulture. New World vultures include the turkey vulture, the black vulture, the California condor, and the Andean condor.

Though these birds are alike, they're not part of the same family. Old World vultures belong to the Accipitridae (ak-suh-PIH-truh-dee) family. New World Vultures belong to the Cathartidae (kuh-THAR-tuh-dee) family. Some scientists disagree over how to group vultures, so this may change in the future.

There are many differences between the two vulture families. Old World vultures use sight to find their food, while New World vultures use their sense of smell. Also, Old World vultures have a voice box for calling, while New World vultures don't—they can only hiss and grunt.

griffon vulture

turkey vulture

Andean condor

California condor

Inside Vulture Habitats

Vultures live in every part of the world except Australia and Antarctica. Old World vultures live in Europe, Asia, and Africa. New World vultures are found in North America and South America.

Vultures live in many kinds of **habitats**. They're commonly found in open country or grasslands that have a lot of open space. They can live in rocky or wooded areas, but they mostly use these places for nesting. Because they're scavengers, vultures like to be in places where they can easily find food.

Vultures will live anywhere, as long as there's food available.

An Odd Bird

There's no mistaking vultures when you see them—these birds are rather odd looking. Vultures' best-known features are their bald head and neck. This may be a helpful **adaptation**. Long feathers would trap flesh, blood, and bacteria from the meat vultures eat, so it's better for them to be bald.

You can also recognize vultures by how they fly. Vultures don't flap their wings much. Instead, they can **soar** and circle the sky for hours just by riding the wind. Many vultures appear to wobble when they're soaring.

Vultures are larger than most birds, and they have a wide **wingspan** that helps them catch and ride the wind until they find a meal.

Spoiled Rotten

Vultures are scavengers, so they'll eat pretty much anything they can find. This is usually carrion, or dead flesh. Sometimes it's spoiled, which means it's rotten! Vultures sometimes eat weak, sick, or young animals, too.

Old World vultures find food using their eyes, but New World vultures find it using their nose. They have a great sense of smell. It's been said they can smell rotting flesh up to 1 mile (1.6 km) away! Once a vulture finds food, it tells other vultures where it is. In just moments, the **carcass** will be surrounded by scavengers.

RAPTOR FACTOR

If a vulture eats too much, it may be too heavy to fly. It can throw up a little bit of its food to feel lighter.

When vultures find food, they eat as much of it as they can. They can store extra food in a pouch called a crop. They eat it later or feed it to their young.

Gross, but Greatly Important

Vultures' bodies are well suited for their rotten dinner. They have a strong **immune system** that keeps them from getting sick when they eat dead or spoiled meat. If people ate what vultures eat, we would get very sick.

Even though vultures' diet may seem gross, what they do is very important. Vultures are kind of like a cleanup crew—they get rid of dead animals, which keeps sicknesses from spreading. If the world didn't have vultures, dead animals would be a more common sight.

RAPTOR FACTOR

In the 1990s, India's vulture population dropped by more than 95 **percent**. Dogs took over scavenging, which caused their population to grow and spread deadly sicknesses.

Every animal in a habitat has an important job. It's vultures' job to get rid of the dead animals.

The Turkey Vulture

The turkey vulture is one of the most common vultures in North America. It's often seen over open country, and it also lives near human habitats. That's because food is easily found in both places.

Turkey vultures' bodies are covered with brown feathers. Their bald head is red, and their legs and feet are pink. They have nose openings on their beak. Turkey vultures have an excellent sense of smell. They use it to find dead **mammals**, lizards, and sometimes other birds.

RAPTOR FACTOR

Turkey vultures are known to be picky about what they eat. They often just eat the most tender, or soft, meat.

Turkey vultures almost never attack live prey. Their great sense of smell helps them find dead animals, even if they're hidden under plant matter.

The California Condor

The largest flying bird in North America is a vulture. It's the California condor. Its wingspan can be up to 10 feet (3 m) across. Its large size allows it to scavenge large animal carcasses, such as deer and cattle.

The California condor has black feathers with patches of white feathers on its underside. Its bald head can be white or purplish-red, but the color can change if it's scared or excited. After feeding on carrion, the California condor cleans its head by rubbing it in the grass or on tree branches.

California condors are endangered, which means their population is in danger of dying out. Today, they live only in California, Arizona, a part of Mexico, and zoos.

Decide for Yourself

Vultures have gained a bad reputation because they're scavengers. Some people think vultures are a sign of death or **doom**. Not many people enjoy seeing vultures rip apart a dead animal.

However unsettling this may be, vultures are just doing their job. Instead of seeing them as scary, many people see them as important. They play a big part in keeping our planet clean and free of sicknesses. Which side are you on?

Glossary

adaptation: A change that helps an animal survive.

carcass: The dead body of an animal.

doom: Something terrible.

habitat: The natural home of a person, animal, or plant.

immune system: Processes of the body that work to keep it healthy and fight off sicknesses.

mammal: A warm-blooded animal that has a backbone and hair, and feeds milk to its young.

percent: Part of a whole.

prey: An animal hunted by other animals for food. Also, to hunt another animal for food.

reputation: The beliefs held about someone or something.

scavenger: An animal that feeds on carrion. "To scavenge" is "to search for carrion as food."

soar: To fly or rise high in the air.

wingspan: The measurement from the tip of one wing to the tip of the other.

Index

Websites